1864

ADDY'S COOK BOOK

*A Peek at
Dining in the
Past with Meals
You Can Cook Today*

PLEASANT COMPANY PUBLICATIONS, INC.

Published by Pleasant Company Publications
For information, address: Book Editor, Pleasant Company Publications,
8400 Fairway Place, P.O. Box 620998, Middleton, WI 53562.

First Edition.
Printed in the United States of America.
95 96 97 98 99 WCR 10 9 8 7 6 5 4

PICTURE CREDITS
The following individuals and organizations have generously
given permission to reprint illustrations in this book:
Page 1—Reproduced from *Back of the Big House: The Architecture of Plantation Slavery*,
by John Michael Vlach. Copyright 1993 by The University of North Carolina Press;
3—Taken from *Grandma's Tea Leaf Ironstone, A History and Study of English and
American Potteries*, by Annise Doring Heaivilin, © 1981 (bottom); 5—Taken from
Old Cookbooks, An Illustrated History by Eric Quayle, E.P. Dutton, NY, © 1978;
6—Collection Old Slave Mart Museum, Judith Wragg Chase, Director; 7—Antique
Stove and Tin Museum, Manchester, Vermont; 11—Amistad Collection; 13—Library of
Congress; 16—The Bettmann Archive; 17—North Wind Picture Archives; 23—Library
of Congress; 25—Cook Collection, Valentine Museum, Richmond, Virginia; 27—The
Metropolitan Museum of Art. Morris K. Jesup Fund, 1940; 28—Savannah, Georgia:
Beehive Press, 1973; 29—Photographs and Prints Division, Schomburg Center for
Research in Black Culture, The New York Public Library, Astor, Lenox and
Tilden Foundations; 30—The Bettman Archive; 31—From *The Rise and Decline of
the Great Atlantic & Pacific Tea Company*, by William I. Walsh. Copyright © 1986
by William I. Walsh. Reprinted by arrangement with Carol Publishing Group.
A Lyle Stuart Book; 33—Taken from *Colonial Kitchens, Their Furnishings,
and Their Gardens* by Frances Phipps; 43—The Bettman Archive;
44—National Commission for Museums and Monuments, Nigeria.

Edited by Jodi Evert
Written by Rebecca Sample Bernstein,
Terri Braun, Tamara England, and Jodi Evert
Designed and Art Directed by Jane S. Varda
Produced by Karen Bennett, Laura Paulini, and Pat Tuchscherer
Cover and Inside Illustrations by Susan Mahal
Photography by Mark Salisbury
Historical and Picture Research by Polly Athan, Rebecca Sample Bernstein,
Terri Braun, Jodi Evert, and Doreen Smith
Recipe Testing Coordinated by Jean doPico
Food Styling by Janice Bell
Prop Research by Leslie Cakora

Library of Congress Cataloging-in-Publication Data

Addy's cookbook : a peek at dining in the past with meals you can cook today /
[edited by Jodi Evert ; written by Rebecca Sample Bernstein . . . et al. ; inside
illustrations by Susan Mahal ; photography by Mark Salisbury]. — 1st ed.
p. cm.
ISBN 1-56247-123-6 (softcover)
1. Cookery—Juvenile literature. 2. Afro-American cookery—Juvenile literature.
3. United States—History—Civil War, 1861-1865—Juvenile literature. 4. United
States—Social life and customs—19th century—Juvenile literature. [1. Afro-American
cookery. 2. Cookery, American. 3. Slavery. 4. United States—Social life and
customs—19th century.] I. Bernstein, Rebecca Sample. II. Evert, Jodi.
III. Mahal, Susan, ill. IV. Salisbury, Mark, ill.
TX652.5.A35   1994   641.5'123—dc20   94-25071   CIP   AC

CONTENTS

Special thanks to all the children and adults who tested the recipes and gave us their valuable comments:

Maretta Babler and her mother Margot Babler
Amie Bergquist and her mother Tari Bergquist
Alisa Brown and her mother Marlene Brown
Emily Dresen and her mother Mary Jo Dresen
Michelle Endres and her mother Brenda Endres
Amanda Ganser and her mother Tam Ganser
Heidi Ganser and her mother Marie Ganser
Ashley Holekamp and her mother Lynda Holekamp
Amanda Keller and her mother Sharon Keller
Christine Klein and her mother Beverly Klein
Cassie and Tory Lee and their mother Debra Lee
Marianna March and her mother Donna March
Melissa Martin and her mother Jeanette Martin
Mallory Mason and her mother Janet Mason
Rebecca Russell and her mother Kathleen Russell
Tara Salbego and her mother Monica Schober
Katie Scallon and her mother Betsy Scallon
Paula Simons and her mother Janis Simons
Brenna Skelly and her mother Theresa Skelly
Vanessa Theis and her mother LaVonne Theis
Rebecca Theisen and her mother Deanna Theisen
Kristi Wendtland and her mother Jeanne Wendtland
Emily Ziegler and her mother Susan Ziegler

COOKING IN THE CIVIL WAR

I n Addy's time, many African Americans were forced to live as slaves on plantations in the South. Many slaves spent their days planting, tending, and harvesting food in their owners' fields or preparing food for their owners' tables. Others were craftspeople like carpenters and seamstresses.

Each enslaved person was usually allowed about three pounds of bacon and six quarts of cornmeal each week. Families tried to stretch this small amount of food in any way they could. If they could find the time, they fished, grew vegetables of their

A woman beside her cooking fireplace.

own, and cooked savory stews and sauces from simple ingredients. They also learned to recognize the berries, nuts, and herbs found in the woods near the plantation.

ADDY ☀ 1864

In 1864, Addy Walker and her mother escaped to freedom in the North after their family was torn apart by slavery. They brought many southern cooking traditions with them when they came to live in Philadelphia.

Some enslaved people like Addy and her mother escaped to freedom in the northern states. They arrived with almost nothing. Newly freed slaves might have their first meals in the North with church groups or other people who opposed slavery, called *abolitionists*. The groups also helped them find jobs and places to live. When these freed slaves were settled, they gave their time and money to help other people in slavery take their freedom.

Learning about cooking in the past will help you understand what it was like to grow up the way Addy did. Cooking the meals she ate will bring history alive for you and your family today.

KITCHENS IN THE 1860S

BANKING THE FIRE

*To keep the fires in their cabins from going out at night, enslaved people **banked** the coals, or almost covered them with ashes. In the morning, they stirred the ashes. Underneath, the coals were still hot enough to start a fire to make breakfast.*

KEEPING FOOD COLD

*In Addy's time, kitchens didn't have refrigerators. Some foods—like meat, milk, and butter—spoil if they aren't kept cold. So cooks in Addy's time had to get these foods fresh and use them up quickly. A few people had an early kind of refrigerator called an **ice box**, like the one shown here, where large blocks of ice kept foods chilled.*

Addy sometimes helped Auntie Lula in the brick kitchen building on Master Stevens's plantation. But the food Auntie Lula cooked there was only for Master Stevens and his family. Slave families didn't have kitchens. They cooked their food in small fireplaces in their one-room cabins. They never put the fire out, not even in the hottest weather, because it was hard to restart and it was needed both for cooking and for light.

A kitchen building.

In the garret above Mrs. Ford's dress shop, Addy and Momma cooked on a coal-burning stove made of cast iron. It was easier to cook on the stove than in a fireplace. The stove heated foods much more quickly and evenly because less of the heat was lost up the chimney or into the open room. Addy had to be careful not to brush up against the hot cast iron, though. It could burn a hole right through her skirt!

When Addy and her family moved into Mr. and Mrs. Golden's boarding house, Mrs. Golden cooked all the meals. She had a whole room for a kitchen. It had a big table for preparing meals, and cupboards and shelves for storing pots, pans, and dishes. In the winter, her kitchen was warm and cozy. But in the summer, it was too hot to be comfortable. Some wealthy families in Addy's time had two kitchens—one on the main floor to keep the house warm in the winter, and a summer kitchen in a cooler place, such as the basement.

SETTING ADDY'S TABLE

In their tiny cabin on Master Stevens's plantation, Addy and her family ate at a sturdy table that Poppa had made from wood scraps. He sanded the rough boards until the table had a smooth, even finish. Poppa carved a few wooden plates and spoons for the family, too. They also had bowls made from dried gourds and a few tin cups.

When Addy and Momma lived in the garret, their only furniture was a bed and a small table with two chairs. They prepared and ate their meals at the table. After dinner, the table was a good spot for Addy to do her homework and for Momma to sew. Momma used some of her wages from sewing dresses in Mrs. Ford's shop to buy a few dishes. She and Addy bought spoons, knives, and ceramic dishes at Mr. Delmonte's Secondhand Shop.

At Mr. and Mrs. Golden's boarding house, Addy sometimes helped Mrs. Golden set the table for dinner. Mrs. Golden had enough dishes and silverware for all the boarders who lived there. On Sundays and for special dinners, Mrs. Golden asked Addy to set the table with beautiful lavender glasses. Addy had never seen a prettier table. It looked like it was dressed for a party!

NAPKINS AND NAPKIN RINGS

In Addy's day, people used cloth napkins that could be as large as one square yard! Everyday napkins weren't washed after each meal. Instead, people put their napkins in napkin rings to store them neatly between meals. At boarding houses, the napkin rings had numbers so boarders knew which napkin was theirs.

TEA LEAF CHINA

*One of the most popular china patterns in Addy's time was called **Tea Leaf**. It gets its name from the simple, elegant tea leaf design applied in a copper or gold color to each dish. This tableware was made of **ironstone**, a sturdy, practical type of pottery.*

TIPS FOR TODAY'S COOKS

MEASURING FLOUR

A good cook measures exactly. Here is a hint for measuring flour. Spoon the flour into a measuring cup, heaping it up over the top. Then use the spoon handle to level off the flour. Don't shake or tap the cup.

TABLE OF MEASUREMENTS

3 teaspoons = 1 tablespoon
2 cups = 1 pint
2 pints = 1 quart
4 cups = 1 quart

You'll find below a list of things that every good cook should know. But this is the most important tip: **work with an adult.** This is the safe way for you to work in the kitchen. Cooking together is fun, too. It's a tradition American families have always shared. Keep it alive today!

1. Choose a time that suits you and the adult who's cooking with you, so that you will both enjoy working together in the kitchen.

2. Wash your hands with soap before you handle food. Wear an apron, tie back your hair, and roll up your sleeves.

3. Read a recipe carefully, all the way through, before you start it. Look at the pictures. They will help you understand the steps.

4. Gather all the ingredients and equipment you will need before you start to cook. Put everything where you can reach it easily.

5. Ask an adult to show you how to peel, cut, or grate with sharp kitchen tools. Always use a chopping board to save kitchen counters.

6. Pay attention while using knives so that you don't cut your fingers! Remember, a good, sharp knife is safer than a dull one.

7. When you stir or mix, hold the bowl or pan steady on a flat surface, not in your arms.

8. Make sure your mixing bowls, pots, and pans are the right size. If they are too small, you'll probably spill. If pots and pans are too large, foods will burn more easily.

9. Clean up spills right away.

10. Pots and pans will be less likely to spill on the stove if you turn the handles toward the side.

11. Have an adult handle hot pans. Don't use the stove burners or the oven without permission or supervision.

12. Turn off the burner or the oven as soon as a dish is cooked.

13. Potholders and oven mitts will protect you from burns. Use them when you touch anything hot. Protect kitchen counters by putting trivets or cooling racks under hot pots and pans.

14. Keep hot foods hot and cold foods cold. If you plan to make things early and serve them later, store them properly. Foods that could spoil belong in the refrigerator. Wrap foods well.

15. If you decide to make a whole meal, be sure to plan so that all the food will be ready when you are ready to serve it.

16. Cleanup is part of cooking, too. Leave the kitchen at least as clean as you found it. Wash all the dishes, pots, and pans. Sweep the floor. Throw away the garbage.

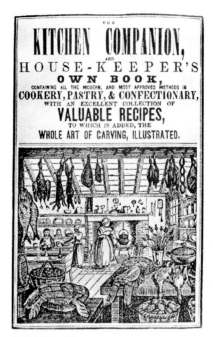

1860s COOKBOOKS

Cookbooks in Addy's time were very different from cookbooks today. Since some people had stoves and some didn't, cookbooks gave instructions for cooking in a fireplace and on a stove. Instead of telling how long to cook a dish, recipes told cooks to "fry until golden brown" or "simmer the water to half a pint."

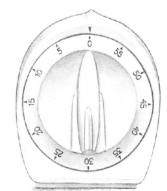

TIMING

When a recipe gives two cooking times—for example, when it says, "bake 25 to 30 minutes"—first set the timer for the shorter time. If the food is not done when the timer rings, give it more time.

BREAKFAST

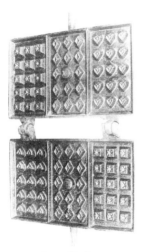

A waffle iron.

In Addy's time, poor families didn't usually eat big breakfasts. They didn't have much money to spend on food, and they didn't have much time to make breakfast. Some mothers and fathers who lived in the city had to be at work by 6:00 A.M., and often they worked past suppertime.

When Addy and Momma lived in the garret above Mrs. Ford's shop, they made breakfast foods that were simple and inexpensive. Most mornings they crumbled cornbread left over from dinner into a bowl and poured buttermilk on top. On cold mornings, they took time to make warm, filling breakfast foods like buttermilk biscuits and hominy grits. *Hominy* is corn kernels with the hulls taken off. When hominy is ground into cereal, it's called *grits*. Breakfast foods like scrambled eggs or pork sausage and gravy would have been very special treats for Addy.

When Poppa was finally able to get to Philadelphia, Addy and Momma wanted to celebrate their first day of being together again. They got up before sunrise and started making a breakfast of grits and fried apples. Addy and Momma worked quietly so they wouldn't wake Poppa. He was very tired from his long journey to freedom.

Addy scooped a little coal over the glowing embers inside the stove. Then she used the tin dipper to break through the thin layer of ice on top of the water bucket. She poured a few dippers of water into the skillet on top of the stove. While the water heated for the grits, Addy helped Momma slice the apples. Poppa woke up when he smelled the apples frying. When Addy saw the smile on Poppa's face,

A stove from Addy's time.

she knew that their first day together in freedom was starting out just right.

BREAKFAST

☀

Hominy Grits

•

Pork Sausage and Gravy

•

Buttermilk Biscuits

•

Fried Apples

•

Scrambled Eggs

HOMINY GRITS

Grits is the name for a cereal
made from coarsely ground corn.

INGREDIENTS

4 cups water
1 cup quick grits
Butter to grease casserole
2 eggs
½ cup heavy cream
1 teaspoon salt
¼ teaspoon pepper

EQUIPMENT

Measuring cups
 and spoons
2-quart saucepan
 with lid
Wooden spoon
1½-quart casserole dish
Medium mixing bowl
Small mixing bowl
Large mixing bowl
Wire whisk or eggbeater
Potholders
Trivet

DIRECTIONS   *6 servings*

1. Measure the water into the saucepan. Turn the heat to high until the water *boils*, or bubbles rapidly.

2. Stir the grits completely into the boiling water. Cover the saucepan and cook over low heat for 5 minutes. Then remove the pan from the heat and set the cooked grits aside to cool.

3. While the grits are cooling, preheat the oven to 350°. Grease the casserole dish with butter.

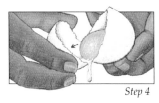

Step 4

4. Ask an adult to help you separate the egg whites from the egg yolks as shown. The egg whites should fall into the medium mixing bowl. Put the egg yolks into the small mixing bowl.

5. Measure 2 cups of cooled grits into the large mixing bowl. Beat them with the wooden spoon until they are smooth.

Step 5

6. Beat the egg yolks with the wooden spoon. Then stir them into the grits. Add the cream, salt, and pepper.

7. Use the wire whisk or eggbeater to whip the egg whites until they form stiff peaks, approximately 5 minutes.

Step 7

8. Gently stir the egg whites into the grits mixture until they are well blended.

9. Spoon the mixture into the casserole dish. Bake for 1$\frac{1}{2}$ hours.

10. When the top is golden brown, have an adult remove the grits from the oven. Place the casserole dish on a trivet at the table and serve. ☀

THE GOLD OF THE SOUTH

*Corn was a **staple**, or main food, of most people living in the South. Many Southerners said that people who had corn had everything. Both people and animals could eat corn, and kernels of corn could be planted to grow more! One woman wrote, "In the South, corn is more valuable than gold."*

PORK SAUSAGE AND GRAVY

To Southerners in Addy's time, fatback, sowbelly, and middlin' were all names of different cuts of pork.

INGREDIENTS

1½ pounds country-style
   pork sausage links
⅓ cup flour
1 cup water
1 cup milk
1 cup heavy cream
Salt and pepper to taste

EQUIPMENT

Large skillet
Tongs
Ovenproof serving plate
Tinfoil
Potholders
Measuring cups
Wooden spoon
Gravy boat or
   serving bowl

DIRECTIONS   *6 servings*

1. Put the sausage links in the skillet and turn on the burner to medium.

2. Fry the sausage links for 15 to 20 minutes, turning them often with the tongs.

3. When the sausage links are browned on all sides, use the tongs to put them on the serving plate. Cover the plate with tinfoil and set it aside or put it in a warm *(180°)* oven.

4. Have an adult remove all but ⅓ cup of the drippings from the skillet.

5. Sprinkle the flour over the drippings in the skillet and stir quickly over medium heat.

6. Add the water a little at a time, stirring quickly and constantly to keep the mixture from getting lumpy.

Step 2

7. When all the water has been added and the mixture is smooth, add the milk, cream, salt, and pepper.

8. Turn up the heat to medium high. Continue stirring the gravy until it begins to bubble and thicken. Add more salt and pepper if needed. Turn off the heat.

9. Have an adult pour the gravy from the skillet into a gravy boat or serving bowl and place it on the table.

10. If the sausages are in the oven, have an adult take them out. Remove the tinfoil from the plate and serve. Spoon or pour the gravy over hot buttermilk biscuits *(page 12).* ☀

CHITLINS AND CRACKLINGS

When a hog was butchered in Addy's day, no part of it was wasted. People ate **chitlins***, made from the small intestines of pigs, and* **cracklings***, which is pigskin fried until crispy brown. People still eat chitlins and cracklings today.*

BUTTERMILK BISCUITS

Many families in Addy's day ate light, flaky buttermilk biscuits at every meal!

INGREDIENTS

2 cups flour
4 teaspoons baking
  powder
3/4 teaspoon salt
4 tablespoons shortening
  or lard
2/3 cup buttermilk
Extra flour for cutting
  board and rolling pin

EQUIPMENT

Flour sifter
Medium mixing bowl
Measuring cups
  and spoons
Wooden spoon
Pastry cutter
Cutting board
Rolling pin
2- to 3-inch round cookie
  cutter or drinking glass
Cookie sheet
Potholders
Spatula
Serving plate

DIRECTIONS   *12 biscuits*

1. Preheat the oven to 375°.

Step 2

2. Put the flour sifter into the mixing bowl. Measure the flour, baking powder, and salt into the sifter. Then sift them into the bowl.

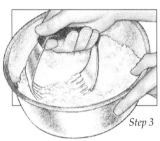
Step 3

3. Add the shortening or lard by spoonfuls. Use the pastry cutter to cut in the shortening until the mixture becomes a coarse meal.

4. Stir the buttermilk into the mixture to make a soft ball of dough.

Step 5

5. Sprinkle extra flour on the cutting board. Put the ball of dough on the board. Knead the dough about 6 times by pressing down and folding it in half.

6. Sprinkle more flour on the board and place the ball of dough in the center. Pat down the dough until it is flat.

7. Put a little flour on the rolling pin. Gently roll the dough from the center to the edges until it is ¹/2 inch thick.

Step 7

8. Use the cookie cutter or the glass to cut out the biscuits.

Step 8

9. Put the biscuits on the cookie sheet and bake them for 10 to 12 minutes, until they start to turn golden brown.

10. Have an adult remove the biscuits from the oven. Let them cool for a minute, and then use a spatula to move the biscuits to a serving plate. Serve them hot with pork sausage and gravy *(page 10).* ☀

BUTTERMILK

*This girl is churning butter just the way Addy did. Most people in slavery did not get many dairy products. Some plantation owners did allow slaves to have **buttermilk**, the liquid left over after milk is churned into butter. Buttermilk became one of the main sources of calcium in the diet of slaves.*

FRIED APPLES

Fried apples make a hot, sweet breakfast treat!

INGREDIENTS

4 firm apples
1/4 cup water
1/3 cup butter
1/3 cup packed light-
   brown sugar
2 tablespoons lemon juice

EQUIPMENT

Apple corer
Sharp knife
Cutting board
Measuring cups
   and spoon
Large skillet with lid
Spatula
Serving dish

DIRECTIONS   *4-6 servings*

1. Wash the apples well with cold water.

Step 2

2. Insert the apple corer into the center of each apple and twist it to cut around the core. Remove the cores from all the apples.

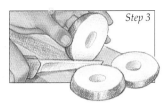
Step 3

3. Have an adult help you slice the apples into 1/2-inch rings on the cutting board.

4. Measure the water and butter into the skillet. Warm them over medium heat until the butter melts.

Step 5

5. Add the apple slices to the skillet. Cook them for about 10 minutes. Turn them once or twice with the spatula while they cook.

6. Sprinkle the brown sugar and lemon juice over the slices. Gently turn all the slices to mix.

7. Cover the skillet and remove it from the heat. Let the apples sit for 10 minutes, and serve. ☀

SCRAMBLED EGGS

INGREDIENTS

3 green onions *(optional)*
6 eggs
Salt and pepper
2 tablespoons sausage
   drippings or butter
1 tablespoon water

EQUIPMENT

Paring knife
Cutting board
Small mixing bowl
Wire whisk or fork
Skillet
Wooden spoon

Children like Addy often had the job of collecting eggs on plantations in the South.

DIRECTIONS   *6 servings*

1. If you are including green onions, wash them in cold water. Cut off the root ends and peel off the outer skin. If you are not including the onions, start with step 3.

2. Slice the white ends and the green stems of the onions into $1/2$-inch pieces.

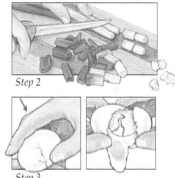
Step 2

3. Crack the eggs into the mixing bowl. Beat them until they are well mixed, using the wire whisk or fork. Add a *dash*, or a small amount, of salt and pepper.

Step 3

4. Warm the sausage drippings or butter and water in the skillet over medium heat.

5. Add the green onions to the skillet and stir them as they cook. They are done when the white ends become clear.

6. Pour the eggs into the skillet. Stir them gently while they cook. When they are thick and creamy, they're ready to eat.

RAISING CHICKENS

Many people in slavery raised their own chickens. They rarely butchered their chickens because they wanted to sell the eggs for extra money or cook them for their own families.

15

DINNER

When Addy and her parents moved into Mr. and Mrs. Golden's boarding house, part of their rent paid for their meals. Mrs. Golden did the cooking at the boarding house. She rang a bell to let all the boarders know when a meal was ready. Then everyone went to the dining room to eat together.

Sometimes when Addy came home from school and all the other boarders were at work, Mrs. Golden let Addy help with dinner. Addy loved to get flour, sugar, and cornmeal from the wooden barrels Mrs. Golden kept in the pantry. When Mrs. Golden made fried fish for dinner, she always made deep-fried cornmeal dumplings, called *hush puppies*, too. She made them by adding milk, an egg, and a little bit of onion to some of the fish batter. Mrs. Golden said that fried fish and hush puppies went together like morning and sunrise. No one should have one without the other!

On New Year's Day, Addy and Momma made a special dish called *Hoppin' John* to share with everyone at the boarding house. Hoppin' John was a mixture of black-eyed peas, rice, and bacon. When Addy and her family lived on Master Stevens's plantation, Auntie Lula made Hoppin' John every New Year's Day. She said that eating humble food like Hoppin' John on New Year's Day would bring good fortune for the year ahead.

Addy wondered if Auntie Lula would be making Hoppin' John this New Year's Day, too. She hoped that Auntie Lula, Uncle Solomon, and her baby sister Esther were still safe, living together on the plantation. It made Addy feel closer to them to think that they might all be enjoying the same food on the same day. She hoped Hoppin' John would work its magic and bring them all together again.

DINNER

☀

Corn Pudding

•

Hoppin' John

•

Fried Fish

•

Hush Puppies

•

Sweet Potato Pone

CORN PUDDING

Serve creamy corn pudding while it's still steaming from the oven.

INGREDIENTS

Butter to grease
    casserole dish
3 eggs
2 cups corn *(fresh or frozen)*
¼ cup flour
½ teaspoon salt
¼ teaspoon pepper
2 tablespoons butter
1 cup milk
1 cup cream

EQUIPMENT

9 x 12-inch baking pan
2-quart casserole dish
Medium mixing bowl
Fork or wire whisk
Measuring cups
    and spoons
Wooden spoon
Small saucepan
Knife
Potholders
Trivet

DIRECTIONS　　*6-8 servings*

1. Fill the baking pan with an inch of water and set it in the oven. Preheat the oven to 325°.

2. Grease the casserole dish with butter. Set it aside.

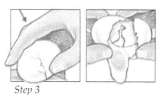
Step 3

3. Crack the eggs into the mixing bowl as shown. Beat them with the fork or wire whisk until bubbles form on the top.

Step 4

4. If you are using fresh corn, cut it from the cob as shown. If you are using frozen corn, run the bag under cold water to separate the kernels.

5. Stir the corn into the eggs. Sprinkle the flour, salt, and pepper over the eggs and corn. Then mix them in.

6. Melt 2 tablespoons of butter in the saucepan over low heat.

7. Add the melted butter, milk, and cream to the corn mixture. Stir.

8. Pour the corn mixture into the greased casserole dish.

9. Have an adult put the casserole dish into the baking dish of water in the oven.

10. Bake the corn pudding for 1 hour and 15 minutes, or until a knife inserted into the center comes out clean.

11. Have an adult remove the casserole dish from the oven. Set the corn pudding on a trivet at the table and serve it warm. ☀

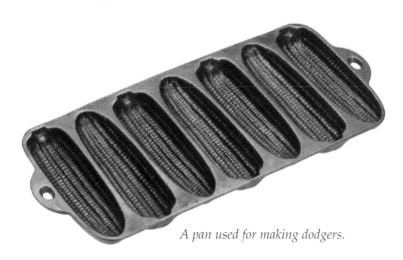

A pan used for making dodgers.

DODGERS AND SCRATCHBACKS

*In Addy's time, cornmeal was cooked in many different ways. **Dodgers** were cornmeal cakes baked so hard that if they were thrown, it was a good idea to dodge them! To make **scratchbacks**, cooks dropped spoonfuls of cornmeal batter into a buttered tin. When baked, scratchbacks had rough, scratchy tops.*

HOPPIN' JOHN

Beans and rice together were a good source of protein for Addy, and they still are for you today!

INGREDIENTS

6 slices bacon
2 cups water
1 16-ounce package frozen
  black-eyed peas
1 cup rice
1 teaspoon salt
¼ teaspoon pepper

EQUIPMENT

Paper towels
Skillet
Tongs
Measuring cup
  and spoons
3-quart saucepan with lid
Wooden spoon
Serving bowl

DIRECTIONS   *6 servings*

1. Place 2 layers of paper towels on the counter next to the stove. Separate the bacon strips and place them side by side in the skillet.

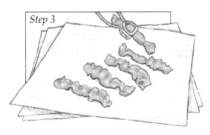
Step 2

2. Turn the heat to medium high. Have an adult help you cook the bacon until the edges start to curl. Use the tongs to turn each slice to the other side. Continue cooking, turning the slices frequently.

3. When the bacon is golden brown and crisp, lift it out of the skillet and put it on the paper towels to cool and drain. Save the bacon drippings in the skillet.

4. Measure the water into the saucepan. Turn the heat to high.

5. When the water *boils*, or bubbles rapidly, have an adult help you add the black-eyed peas and rice to the water. Stir well.

6. Stir in the salt, pepper, and 2 tablespoons of the bacon drippings.

7. Let the water come to a boil again. Then turn the heat down to low.

8. Cover the saucepan and cook the Hoppin' John about 20 to 25 minutes, until the black-eyed peas and rice are tender. The water should be absorbed into the mixture.

9. Crumble the bacon with your fingers and stir it into the rice and black-eyed peas.

10. Spoon the Hoppin' John into a bowl and serve. ☀

WHO WAS HOPPIN' JOHN?

There are different stories about how Hoppin' John got its name. One story says that a man named John "came a-hoppin'" whenever his wife cooked it. Another story says that children always hopped around the table before this dish was served. Yet another story says that it was named after a lively waiter who served this dish.

Step 9

BLACK-EYED PEAS

A black-eyed pea is a light brown pea with a small black dot on it. These peas were brought to America from Africa in the 1600s, when the slave trade began.

FRIED FISH

Crispy fried fish tastes great with a crunchy cornmeal batter.

INGREDIENTS

6 pieces of fresh fish fillet
  (Catfish is traditional.)
1 cup white cornmeal
1/2 cup flour
1 teaspoon salt
1/2 teaspoon pepper
Vegetable oil

EQUIPMENT

Paper towels
Measuring cups
  and spoons
Paper lunch bag
Wax paper
Large heavy skillet
Potholders
Spatula
Fork
Serving plate

DIRECTIONS   *6 servings*

1. Rinse the pieces of fish in cold water and dry them gently with paper towels.

Step 2

2. Measure the cornmeal, flour, salt, and pepper into the paper bag. Hold the top of the bag closed and shake it to mix the ingredients.

3. Put a sheet of wax paper on the counter near the stove. Put 5 layers of paper towels next to the wax paper.

4. Put a piece of fish in the paper bag. Hold the top closed and shake the bag gently to coat the fish with the cornmeal mixture.

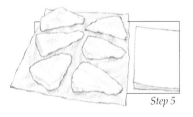
Step 5

5. Take the fish out of the bag and lay it on the wax paper. Prepare the rest of the fish in the same way.

6. Pour about ½ inch of vegetable oil into the skillet. Heat the oil over medium-high heat.

7. When the oil is hot and rippling, have an adult help you gently add the fish to the skillet, using the spatula.

8. Fry the fish on 1 side for 3 to 4 minutes. Then have an adult use the spatula to turn the pieces over. Fry them for another 3 to 4 minutes. The pieces will flake apart with a fork when they are cooked.

9. Use the spatula to lift the fried fish out of the skillet and lay them on the paper towels.

Step 9

10. After the pieces have drained, place them on a plate. Serve with hush puppies *(page 24)*. ☀

FISHING

Enslaved African Americans often fished for extra food to feed their families. Since many plantations were built near a river, some slaves were allowed to fish when they weren't working. Fishing was relaxing, too. It was a peaceful, quiet end to a long workday.

HUSH PUPPIES

Hush puppies and fried fish are a perfect dinnertime combination!

INGREDIENTS

1 small onion
1½ cups white cornmeal
½ cup flour
2 teaspoons baking
  powder
½ teaspoon salt
1 egg
¾ cup milk
2 to 3 cups shortening

EQUIPMENT

Cutting board
Knife
Measuring cups
  and spoons
Large mixing bowl
Mixing spoon
Medium mixing bowl
Fork
Paper towels
Deep-fat fryer or deep,
  heavy skillet
Slotted spoon
Potholders
Serving plate

DIRECTIONS *18 hush puppies*

Step 1

1. Have an adult help you peel and cut the onion into tiny pieces. Set the onion aside.

2. Measure the cornmeal, flour, baking powder, and salt into the large mixing bowl. Stir them together.

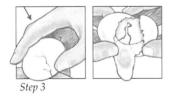
Step 3

3. Crack the egg into the medium mixing bowl and beat it with the fork until it is well mixed.

4. Add the onion pieces and milk to the egg. Mix well.

5. Stir the egg, milk, and onion pieces into the cornmeal and flour mixture.

6. Put 5 layers of paper towels on the counter next to the deep-fat fryer or stove.

7. Melt the shortening in the deep-fat fryer or skillet over medium-high heat. The melted shortening should be 2 to 3 inches deep.

8. Have an adult help you with the next steps. When the shortening is hot, drop the batter into the pan. Use 1 heaping teaspoon of batter for each hush puppy. You can fry 5 or 6 hush puppies at once.

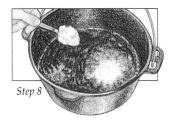

Step 8

9. The hush puppies will sink into the hot shortening. Then they will rise to the top. After 1 to 2 minutes, the hush puppies will be golden brown.

10. Use the slotted spoon to remove the hush puppies. Let them drain on the paper towels.

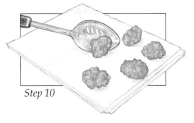

Step 10

11. Add the next batch of batter. Follow steps 8 through 10 until all the hush puppies are fried. Put the hush puppies on the plate and serve them with fried fish *(page 22)*! ☀

Men fishing in the 1890s just as people fished in Addy's time.

"HUSH, PUPPY!"

Where did the hush puppy get its name? One story is that men often took their dogs along when they went fishing. As the men fried the fish they caught, the dogs got hungry and started barking. To quiet them, the men fried cornmeal batter without any fish in it and fed it to the dogs, saying, "Hush, puppy!"

SWEET POTATO PONE

*The word **pone** comes from the Algonquian Indian word **appone**, a cake baked near the fire.*

INGREDIENTS

1-pound sweet potato
Butter to grease
  baking pan
$\frac{1}{4}$ cup butter
$\frac{1}{3}$ cup brown sugar
$\frac{1}{3}$ cup maple or
  corn syrup
$\frac{1}{3}$ cup milk
2 eggs
$\frac{1}{2}$ teaspoon allspice
$\frac{1}{2}$ teaspoon cinnamon
$\frac{1}{4}$ teaspoon cloves
$\frac{1}{4}$ teaspoon ginger
$\frac{1}{2}$ cup chopped nuts
Heavy cream or
  ice cream *(optional)*

EQUIPMENT

Fork
Potholders
9-inch round or square
  baking pan
Butter knife
Medium mixing bowl
Potato masher
Measuring cups
  and spoons
Small saucepan
Wooden spoon
Small bowl

DIRECTIONS   *6 servings*

1. Wash the sweet potato and prick it with a fork. Then bake it in a 350° oven for an hour, or until a fork pierces it easily.

2. Have an adult remove the sweet potato from the oven. Set it aside until it's cool enough to handle.

3. Keep the oven set at 350°. Grease the baking pan with butter.

4. Use the butter knife to peel the skin from the sweet potato. Cut the sweet potato into 4 pieces and put them in the mixing bowl. Discard the skin.

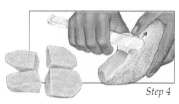

Step 4

5. Mash the sweet potato until it is smooth. You should have about 1 cup of mashed sweet potato.

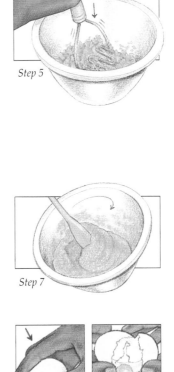

Step 5

6. Melt ¼ cup of butter in the saucepan over low heat. Then stir the butter into the mashed sweet potato.

7. Add the brown sugar, maple or corn syrup, and milk to the sweet potato mixture. Beat until the mixture is smooth.

Step 7

8. Crack the eggs into the small bowl. Beat them with a fork until well mixed. Then stir them into the sweet potato mixture.

Step 8

9. Stir in the allspice, cinnamon, cloves, and ginger. Then add the chopped nuts.

10. Spoon the sweet potato pone into the baking pan and bake for 1 hour. It is done when a knife inserted into the pone comes out clean.

11. Have an adult remove the sweet potato pone from the oven. Serve it warm or cold. Serve it with cream or ice cream if you'd like. ☀

RAISING VEGETABLES

Some families in slavery raised their own vegetables, just as this free family did in the 1870s. They sold some of their vegetables and kept the rest for their own meals. During the winter, they kept their vegetables from freezing by storing them in deep holes dug in the dirt floors of their cabins. The holes were covered with boards.

FAVORITE FOODS

Workers in the late 1800s drawing water from a well.

When enslaved black people escaped to freedom in the North, they brought many of their southern cooking traditions with them. In Philadelphia, Addy and Momma made many of the same foods they had eaten on Master Stevens's plantation in North Carolina, like cornbread and collard greens.

On almost every plantation, each slave received a certain amount of cornmeal each week. The cornmeal was mixed with water to make breads, cakes, and dumplings. Vegetables often were not included in the weekly food supplies given to each slave. Plantation owners sometimes allowed enslaved people to have small vegetable gardens. The vegetables they grew, like collard greens, added much-needed nutrition to their diet. The water the vegetables had been cooked in was called *pot likker*. Slave families dunked cornbread into the pot likker so nothing would go to waste.

When Addy started living in Philadelphia, she began to eat many foods that she and her family didn't have on the plantation. At church socials, she had creamy potato salad and wonderful desserts like juicy peach cobbler. Sometimes Poppa brought the ice cream freezer he had fixed, and all the children took a turn at the crank. Soon there was a taste of sweet homemade ice cream for everyone.

Mother Bethel Church in Philadelphia.

Addy especially loved to help Mrs. Golden make special treats at the boarding house. It was fun to squeeze the juice out of lemon halves to make lemonade and to stir a big bowl full of pound cake batter. Pound cake got its name from the amount of each ingredient that went into it in Addy's time—a pound of flour, a pound of sugar, a pound of eggs, and a pound of butter!

FAVORITE FOODS

☀

Chicken Shortcake

•

Collard Greens

•

Cornbread

•

Potato Salad

•

Lemonade

•

Peach Cobbler

•

Pound Cake

•

Shortbread

CHICKEN SHORTCAKE

Creamy chicken with cornmeal shortcake makes a hearty meal.

INGREDIENTS

Shortcake:
Shortening to grease
  baking pan
1/4 cup shortening or lard
1 cup cornmeal
1 cup flour
1 tablespoon baking
  powder
1 teaspoon sugar
1/4 teaspoon salt
1 egg
1 cup milk or buttermilk

Creamed Chicken:
3 cups cold
  cooked chicken
3 tablespoons butter
3 tablespoons flour
1 1/2 cups milk
1/2 teaspoon salt
1/4 teaspoon pepper

EQUIPMENT

8-inch square baking pan
Measuring cups
  and spoons
Small saucepan
Large mixing bowl
Wooden spoon
Potholders
Knife
Cutting board
Large saucepan
6 plates

DIRECTIONS   *6 servings*

1. Preheat the oven to 425°. Grease the baking pan with shortening and set it in the oven to heat.

2. To make the shortcake batter, melt the lard or shortening in the small saucepan over low heat. Turn off the heat.

3. Measure the cornmeal, flour, baking powder, sugar, and salt into the mixing bowl. Mix them well.

HARDTACK BISCUITS

Hardtack was the bread that soldiers ate every day while they fought in the Civil War. Flour and water was baked into biscuits about three inches square and half an inch thick. Soldiers got about nine or ten of these biscuits a day, and they toasted them, fried them in meat fat, or crumbled them into soups and stews.

4. Add the melted shortening or lard, egg, and milk or buttermilk to the cornmeal mixture.

5. Stir the batter just enough to blend the ingredients. Do not overmix.

GROCERY STORES

Today most people buy food at the grocery store. In 1864, the first grocery store chain opened for business. It was called the Great Atlantic and Pacific Tea Company. You might know it today as the A & P.

6. Have an adult take the baking pan out of the oven. Pour the batter into the pan. Bake the shortcake for 20 minutes.

7. While the shortcake is baking, prepare the chicken. Cut the chicken into small cubes on the cutting board.

Step 7

8. Melt the butter in the large saucepan over medium-low heat.

9. Stir the flour into the melted butter and cook it for a few minutes, stirring constantly.

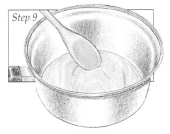

Step 9

10. Slowly pour the milk into the saucepan, stirring constantly.

11. Keep stirring until the mixture is thick and creamy. Add the salt and pepper.

12. Stir in the chicken. Cook over low heat for 5 minutes. Add more milk if the sauce is too thick. To serve, cut the shortcake into squares and spoon the creamed chicken over them. ☀

COLLARD GREENS

Leafy collard greens are best in the autumn, after they've been through a frost.

INGREDIENTS

3 cups water
1 ham hock
3 to 4 bunches
  collard greens
1 tablespoon sugar
1 teaspoon salt
½ teaspoon pepper

EQUIPMENT

Measuring cup
  and spoons
Large cooking pot with lid
Potholders
Serving bowl

DIRECTIONS   *6 servings*

1. Measure the water into the pot. Add the ham hock.

2. Heat the water over high heat until it *boils*, or bubbles rapidly. Turn down the heat. Cover the pot and let the water *simmer*, or bubble gently, for an hour.

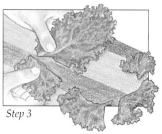

Step 3

3. While the ham hock cooks, wash the collard greens with cold water. Throw away the stems and any yellow leaves. Tear the leaves into bite-sized pieces and set aside.

4. Check the ham hock. If the water has boiled down, add enough water to cover it. Add the greens, sugar, salt, and pepper to the ham hock.

5. Simmer the greens for 45 minutes to an hour, or until they are tender.

6. Have an adult help you pour the collard greens and cooking liquid into a serving bowl. Serve them with cornbread *(next page)*. ☀

CORNBREAD

INGREDIENTS

Shortening to grease
  baking pan
1/4 cup lard or shortening
1 cup cornmeal
1 cup flour
1 tablespoon baking
  powder
1 teaspoon sugar
1/4 teaspoon salt
1 egg
1 cup milk or buttermilk

EQUIPMENT

8-inch square baking pan
Measuring cups
  and spoons
Small saucepan
Large mixing bowl
Wooden spoon
Potholders
Toothpick
Knife

*Use your cornbread to soak up the
pot likker from your collard greens,
just as Addy did.*

DIRECTIONS   *6 servings*

1. Preheat the oven to 425°. Grease the baking
   pan with shortening and heat it in the oven.

2. Melt the lard or shortening in the saucepan
   over low heat. Turn off the heat.

3. Measure the cornmeal, flour, baking powder,
   sugar, and salt into the mixing bowl. Mix well.
   Add the melted lard or shortening, egg, and
   milk or buttermilk. Stir to blend the ingredients.

4. Have an adult take the baking pan out of the
   oven. Pour the batter into the pan and bake for
   20 minutes. The cornbread is done when a toothpick inserted in the middle comes out clean.

5. Have an adult remove the cornbread from the
   oven. Cut it into squares and serve it warm. ☀

CAST-IRON COOKWARE

*In Addy's time, most people
cooked cornbread in cast-
iron skillets. Cast iron
heated the bread evenly
and let it cool slowly so
the bread would have a
nice crisp crust.*

  *A cook **seasoned** a new
cast-iron skillet so foods
wouldn't stick to it. She
rubbed the skillet lightly
with shortening, inside
and out, and then
heated it in a warm
oven for a few hours.*

POTATO SALAD

Addy sometimes helped Mrs. Golden make creamy potato salad for church socials.

INGREDIENTS

6 medium potatoes
2 hard-boiled eggs
½ teaspoon salt
¼ teaspoon pepper
1 teaspoon dry mustard
1 cup mayonnaise
Paprika to sprinkle on top

EQUIPMENT

3-quart saucepan with lid
Slotted spoon
Plate
Knife and cutting board
Large mixing bowl
Measuring cups
   and spoons
Wooden spoon
Serving bowl with lid

DIRECTIONS   *6 servings*

Step 2

Step 3

Step 4

1. Wash the potatoes, and then put them in the saucepan. Add water to cover them.

2. Turn the heat to high until the water *boils*, or bubbles rapidly. Turn the heat to medium low. Cook the potatoes, covered, for 20 minutes. Have an adult help you use the slotted spoon to move the potatoes to the plate.

3. When the potatoes are cool, slice them into small cubes. Put them in the mixing bowl.

4. Crack the eggshells and peel them off. Chop the eggs into tiny pieces. Add them to the mixing bowl. Then mix in the salt, pepper, mustard, and mayonnaise.

5. Spoon the potato salad into the serving bowl. Sprinkle paprika on top. Cover the salad and chill it 2 hours before serving. ☀

LEMONADE

INGREDIENTS

Ice cubes
2 lemons
3 heaping tablespoons
 sugar
Cold water, about 2 cups
Lemon slices to decorate
 glasses

EQUIPMENT

1-quart widemouthed jar
 with lid
Knife and cutting board
Juicer
Small bowl
Measuring spoon
Glasses

When Addy first tasted lemonade, she was surprised that it made her mouth pucker!

DIRECTIONS   *1 quart*

1. Wash the jar in hot, soapy water, and rinse it well. Then fill the jar half full with ice cubes.

2. Cut the lemons in half, as shown.

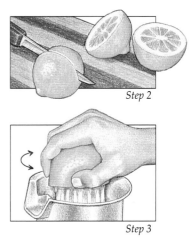
Step 2

Step 3

3. Put the juicer on top of the bowl. Squeeze the juice out of the lemon halves by turning them back and forth on the juicer. Pour the lemon juice into the jar.

4. Add the sugar to the jar. Then fill the jar with cold water. Leave about 1 inch of space at the top of the jar.

5. Put the lid on the jar tightly. Shake the jar to mix the ingredients. The ice cubes will be partly melted.

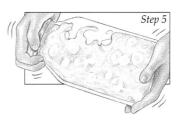
Step 5

6. Pour the lemonade and an ice cube or two into glasses to serve. Drop a thin slice of lemon into each glass for a pretty touch! ☀

PEACH COBBLER

Serve this delicious cobbler warm with a scoop of your favorite ice cream.

INGREDIENTS

Butter to grease skillet or baking pan

Fruit Filling:
4 cups sliced peaches, fresh or frozen
2 tablespoons flour
$\frac{1}{2}$ teaspoon cinnamon
1 cup sugar

Crust:
1 cup flour
1 tablespoon sugar
2 teaspoons baking powder
$\frac{1}{4}$ teaspoon salt
3 tablespoons butter
6 tablespoons half-and-half
Flour for cutting board
1 teaspoon cinnamon
1 tablespoon sugar
1 pint ice cream *(optional)*

EQUIPMENT

10-inch cast-iron skillet or 9-inch square baking pan
Measuring cup and spoons
Large mixing bowl
Wooden spoon
Sifter
Medium mixing bowl
Butter knife
Pastry cutter *(optional)*
Fork
Cutting board
Wax paper
Rolling pin
Cookie cutters
Small bowl
Potholders

DIRECTIONS   *6 servings*

1. Preheat the oven to 425°. Grease the skillet or baking pan with butter.

2. To make the fruit filling, mix the peaches, flour, and cinnamon in the large mixing bowl. Add the sugar a little at a time until the fruit is sweet enough for your taste.

3. Spoon the fruit mixture into the greased skillet or baking pan.

Step 3

4. To make the crust, put the sifter into the medium mixing bowl. Measure the flour, sugar, baking powder, and salt into the sifter. Then sift them into the bowl.

Step 4

5. Cut the butter into small chunks and drop them into the flour mixture. Then use the pastry cutter or fork to cut the butter into the flour mixture until you have pea-sized lumps.

Step 5

6. Add the half-and-half. Stir quickly with the fork just until all the ingredients are moistened.

7. Sprinkle flour on the cutting board. Place the dough on the board. Knead for about 30 seconds. To knead, push down on the dough and then fold it in half. Repeat.

Step 7

8. Sprinkle more flour on your cutting board. Cover the dough with a sheet of wax paper. Roll it out from the center until it is about 1/4 inch thick.

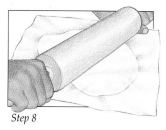

Step 8

9. Cut the crust into shapes with the cookie cutters. Arrange them on top of the fruit.

Step 9

10. Mix the cinnamon and sugar together in the small bowl. Sprinkle the mixture on top of the cobbler. Bake the cobbler for 30 to 35 minutes, or until the crust is browned.

11. Have an adult remove the cobbler from the oven. Let the cobbler cool for about 10 minutes, and serve. Top with ice cream if you'd like. ☀

POUND CAKE

Pound cake topped with fresh berries and ice cream was one of Addy's summertime favorites.

INGREDIENTS

Shortening to grease
  tube pan
Flour to dust greased
  tube pan
6 eggs, room temperature
1 pound butter
  (*4 sticks*), softened
2 cups sugar
2 teaspoons vanilla
3 cups flour
1 teaspoon baking powder
¼ teaspoon salt
Fruit or ice cream (*optional*)

EQUIPMENT

10-inch tube pan
2 large mixing bowls
Small mixing bowl
Wooden spoon
Measuring cup
  and spoons
Wire whisk or eggbeater
Sifter
Medium mixing bowl
Potholders
Serving plate

DIRECTIONS   *1 cake*

1. Preheat the oven to 350°. Grease the bottom and sides of the tube pan. Then lightly coat it with flour, shaking out the excess.

Step 2

2. Have an adult help you separate the egg whites and egg yolks, as shown. Let the egg whites fall into 1 of the large mixing bowls and the egg yolks into the small mixing bowl.

3. Put the butter in the other large mixing bowl. Use the wooden spoon to cut the butter into small chunks.

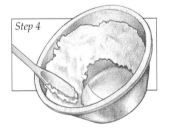
Step 4

4. With the spoon or your clean fingers, press the chunks of butter against the side of the bowl until the butter is very soft and smooth.

5. Mix the sugar into the butter, a little bit at a time. Keep stirring until the butter and sugar are smooth and creamy.

6. Beat the egg yolks until they are well mixed. Then stir them into the butter and sugar and mix well. Add the vanilla.

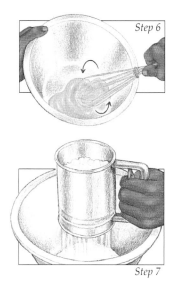

Step 6

7. Put the sifter into the medium mixing bowl. Measure the flour, baking powder, and salt into the sifter. Then sift them into the bowl.

Step 7

8. Add the flour mixture a little at a time to the butter, sugar, and egg yolk mixture. Stir after each addition until the batter is smooth.

9. With a clean whisk or egg beater, beat the egg whites until they are stiff and stand in peaks.

Step 9

10. Gently stir the egg whites into the batter until the whites disappear. Start with $\frac{1}{4}$ of the whites. Gradually add the remaining whites.

11. Spoon the batter gently into the greased and floured tube pan. Bake at 350° for 35 minutes. Then turn down the heat to 325° and bake for another 25 minutes.

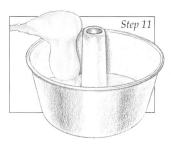

Step 11

12. Have an adult remove the cake from the oven. Let the cake cool in the pan for 10 minutes. Then turn it over onto a serving plate and let the cake cool completely. Serve it plain, with fruit, or with ice cream. ☀

SHORTBREAD

A "short" bread or cake is one that has a lot of butter or shortening in it.

INGREDIENTS

2 cups flour
$\frac{1}{2}$ teaspoon salt
$\frac{1}{2}$ cup brown sugar, packed
1 cup butter (2 sticks), chilled

EQUIPMENT

Sifter
Medium mixing bowl
Measuring cups and spoon
Wooden spoon
Butter knife
Pastry cutter
8-inch square baking pan
Fork
Potholders
Spatula
Serving plate

DIRECTIONS   *16 servings*

1. Preheat the oven to 350°.

Step 2

2. Put the sifter in the mixing bowl. Measure the flour and salt into the sifter and sift them together into the bowl.

3. Be sure the brown sugar is firmly packed into the measuring cup. Then add the brown sugar to the flour and salt and mix well.

4. Add the butter to the mixing bowl. Use the butter knife to cut the butter into small chunks.

Step 5

5. Use the pastry cutter to mix the butter into the flour mixture until you have pea-sized lumps.

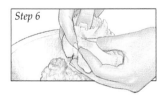
Step 6

6. Wash your hands. Then use your fingertips to work the butter into the flour until the mixture is smooth.

7. Put the shortbread into the baking pan. Press it down with your hands until it is the same thickness everywhere in the pan.

8. Use the fork to prick the shortbread all over.

Step 8

9. Bake the shortbread for 20 minutes. It will turn light brown and pull away from the sides of the pan.

10. Have an adult remove the shortbread from the oven.

11. Use the butter knife to cut the shortbread while it is still warm. Leave it in the pan to cool.

12. When the shortbread has cooled, use the spatula to lift the pieces out and place them on a serving plate. ☀

Step 12

From the book *Addy Learns a Lesson*

COOKING FROM MEMORY

Many people in Addy's time cooked from memory, without using recipes. Instructions for preparing favorite dishes were handed down from one generation to the next by word of mouth.

PLAN AN EMANCIPATION PARTY

FORFEITS

*In Addy's time, people who lost a game paid a **forfeit**, or funny penalty. Write forfeits on slips of paper like those shown above. Put all the slips in a bowl or bag. The person who loses a game picks a slip of paper and has to do what it says!*

The announcement of the Emancipation Proclamation, which freed slaves in most of the South, was cause for celebration in Addy's time, and it's still cause for celebration today! Invite your friends to one of these emancipation parties.

☀ EMANCIPATION CELEBRATION

In Addy's time, people gathered for emancipation celebration church services on New Year's Eve. The tradition began on December 31, 1862, when people waited up all night to hear President Lincoln's Emancipation Proclamation read after it was transmitted over the telegraph wires.

Addy celebrated at a late-night service at her church on New Year's Eve, and at a party the next day. At parties in Addy's time, children often played "Novel Writers," a game that ended up in a funny story. To play, write a sentence that begins a story. Begin writing a second sentence on a new line, but stop in the middle. Fold over the paper so only the unfinished sentence shows. Pass the paper to the next person. She finishes your sentence and writes another. Then she writes half of another sentence, folds over the paper so only the half-sentence shows, and passes the paper to the next person. After everyone has taken a turn, read the whole story aloud!

Games like Blindman's Buff, as it was called in Addy's time, were popular in the 1860s, too. To play, gently blindfold one person and turn her around three times. Everybody else teases the blindfolded person by tickling her with a feather, gently tugging on her clothes, or whispering. If the blindfolded person catches someone and guesses who she is, that person wears the blindfold next.

☀ JUNETEENTH PARTY

On June 19th in 1865, General Gordon Granger announced that all slaves in Texas were free. Even though it was two and a half years after President Lincoln's Emancipation Proclamation, the announcement was cause for celebration. Today, this celebration is called *Juneteenth*, and many Americans celebrate it each summer. Have your Juneteenth party outdoors. Plan a picnic at your favorite park, or just spread a big blanket on the ground in your backyard.

Ice cream was becoming widely popular when Addy was a girl, and people liked to make their own in hand-cranked ice cream freezers. If your family has an ice cream freezer with a hand crank, you and your guests can each take a turn at the crank! Provide a variety of toppings for the ice cream. For example, crush up your favorite cookies or candy bars, and have an adult help you chop nuts. A few hours before the party, cut up fruit and sprinkle lemon juice over it so it won't turn brown. Store the fruit in the refrigerator. Put all the toppings in pretty bowls and let your guests help themselves.

After eating your ice cream, play a party game from Addy's time called Feather. To play, find a small, clean feather. Start the game by tossing the feather in the air and then blowing on it to keep it afloat. When the feather drifts down again, the closest guest blows on it again to keep it from touching the ground. Try to keep the feather afloat for as long as you can!

ICE CREAM FLAVORS

*In Addy's time, people added **extracts**, or concentrated flavorings, to their ice cream while they mixed it in an ice cream freezer. They also used **fruit syrups**, which were made by cutting fruit into thin slices, covering the slices with sugar, and letting a syrup form during a period of a few hours.*

CORNROWS

*The tradition of putting hair in many little braids comes from Africa and is still popular today. After the hairstyle was brought to the United States, it was called **cornrows** because the braids looked like rows of corn in the fields. Some of your guests might like to wear their hair in cornrows for your party.*

Food
Choose recipes from this cookbook to serve at your party. If you host an emancipation celebration on December 31 or January 1, don't forget the Hoppin' John for good luck in the new year! Try the sweet potato pone, peach cobbler, or pound cake with ice cream for a special Juneteenth treat!

Place Settings
Use your everyday dishes for your indoor parties. Pretty paper or plastic plates might be the best choice for a picnic, even though they weren't available in Addy's time.

Clothes
Ask your friends to wear long dresses or skirts if they can. They can also wear aprons or pinafores to protect their clothes. Boys could wear long pants, and all your guests could wear boots.

Decorations
Make simple homemade decorations for your party and set out flags and patriotic banners, just as Addy would have done. If you're having an emancipation celebration on December 31 or January 1, decorate with wreaths and evergreen boughs, too.

Music
Borrow recordings of beautiful spirituals from your local library. Some libraries have recordings of music by the Fisk Jubilee Singers, the first group to bring spirituals to a wide audience. Also look for songs from the Civil War, such as "When Johnny Comes Marching Home."

AMERICAN GIRLS PASTIMES™
Activities from the Past for Girls of Today

You'll enjoy all the Pastimes books about your favorite characters in The American Girls Collection®.

Learn to cook foods that Felicity, Kirsten, Addy, Samantha, and Molly loved with the Pastimes **COOKBOOKS.** They're filled with great recipes and fun party ideas.

Make the same crafts that your favorite American Girls character made. Each of the **CRAFT BOOKS** has simple step-by-step instructions and fascinating historical facts.

Imagine that you are your favorite American Girls character as you stage a play about her. Each of the **THEATER KITS** has four Play Scripts and a Director's Guide.

Learn about fashions of the past as you cut out the ten outfits in each of the **PAPER DOLL KITS.** Each kit also contains a make-it-yourself book plus historical fun facts.

There are **CRAFT KITS** for each character with directions and supplies to make 3 crafts from the Pastimes Craft Books. Craft Kits are available only through Pleasant Company's catalogue, which you can request by filling out the postcard below.

Turn the page to learn more about the other delights in The American Girls Collection. ⟶

I'm an American girl who loves to get mail. Please send me a catalogue of The American Girls Collection®:

My name is _____

My address is _____

City _____ State _____ Zip _____

Parent's signature _____

1961

And send a catalogue to my friend:

My friend's name is _____

Address _____

City _____ State _____ Zip _____

1225

THE AMERICAN GIRLS COLLECTION®

The American Girls Collection tells the stories of five lively nine-year-old girls who lived long ago—Felicity, Kirsten, Addy, Samantha, and Molly. You can read about their adventures in a series of beautifully illustrated books of historical fiction. By reading these books, you'll learn what growing up was like in times past.

There is also a lovable doll for each character with beautiful clothes and lots of wonderful accessories. The dolls and their accessories make the stories of the past come alive today for American girls like you.

The American Girls Collection is for you if you love to curl up with a good book. It's for you if you like to play with dolls and act out stories. It's for you if you want something so special that you will treasure it for years to come.

To learn more about The American Girls Collection, fill out the postcard on the other side of the page and mail it to Pleasant Company, or call **1-800-845-0005.** We will send you a free catalogue about all the books, dolls, dresses, and other delights in The American Girls Collection.